THE CHURCH MEMBER'S MANUAL

THE CHURCH MEMBER'S MANUAL

A Guide to Productive Service in the Local Church

Patrick L. Kelly

Unless otherwise indicated, all Scripture quotations are taken from *The Holy Bible, New King James Version*. Copyright 1982 by Thomas Nelson, Inc.

Some Scripture quotations marked (TEV) have been taken from the *Good News New Testament, Today's English Version* published by the American Bible Society, 1976.

Scripture quotations marked (KJV) are taken from the *King James Version* of the Bible.

ISBN: 978-1-59684-861-0

DEDICATION

This book is dedicated to the congregations that allowed me to shepherd them, and provided the context for the development of the principles and teaching that are presented herein: East Toronto Church of God in Canada, Cathedral of Faith in Bridgeport, Connecticut, and Cathedral Church of God in Deerfield Beach, Florida.

CONTENTS

Acknowledgments 9

Foreword 11

Introduction 13

1. Members Must Support the Church with their Time, Talent, and Treasure 17

2. Members Must Promote the Church through a Godly Influence and Lifestyle Evangelism 29

3. Members Must Defend the Church from External Attack, Internal Disruption, and Spiritual Disease 45

4. Members Must Maintain the Unity of the Fellowship through Submission to Godly Authority and Love for Each Other 63

5. Members Must Honor and Support Pastoral Leaders According to the Bible's Instruction 77

6. Members Must Work in Harmony with the Local Church Vision through Agreement, Alignment, and Assignment 91

7. Members Must Serve and Carry out Duties Primarily for the Glory of God 103

8. Conclusion								113

ACKNOWLEDGMENTS

I am grateful for those who have impacted me and rightfully share in the production of this material: my wife, Nicola, who has been a constant source of encouragement; my daughters, Chayanne and Sela, who are burgeoning writers themselves, and inspire me to chart a path for them to follow; my parents, Levi and Leslin, who exposed me to the things of God and the culture of the church at an early age; and C. Molin, who edited and critiqued this manuscript, and challenged me to think through some of the concepts that are presented in this book.

FOREWORD

Membership in the Christian Church is a unique privilege granted to those who embrace Jesus Christ as their Savior and Lord. They are united with an innumerable host of other believers the world over, and together they comprise the Body of Christ. Localized groups or congregations offer a crystallized membership experience that enables spiritual growth and service in a geographical area where those believers share mutual interests and concerns. Training is usually offered to prepare members for service as lay leaders or clergy, but a guide for general membership responsibilities has rarely, if ever, been presented to congregants.

I was struck by this thought, in the late nineties, as I listened to a teaching series that highlighted the responsibilities of a pastor. I enjoyed the teaching but couldn't help wondering, where was the outlining of expectations and responsibilities of a member? Being unaware of any, I was inspired to develop a sermon series to aid my congregation in understanding the unique role that the member plays in the life and ministry of the church. The emphasis needed to be on responsibilities, since everyone was familiar with the privileges. After prayer and study, seven areas of responsibility emerged and I offered them to my congregation in seven sermons.

During the course of my ministry, I've often encouraged people to write and chronicle their stories for the benefit of others. Some of them have heeded my advice and become published authors. Many have asked me when I would publish something to share my gifts with the world. In 2011, I finally decided to format the series on church membership into a manuscript for publication. After working on it for several months and having it edited and critiqued, I sat on it for several years.

To my surprise, several books on church membership, by notable authors, came out in the interim. It seemed to me that God must have impressed us at the same time to speak to this issue in a published format, but I had hesitated in offering my work. I remain convinced that I offer a different, yet needed, perspective on this issue. Therefore, I present this information in the humble hope that it will make a positive impact upon those members and congregations who will read and apply it.

INTRODUCTION

Ask any church member what the job of a pastor entails, and you will no doubt receive a litany of responses that include preaching, praying for the sick, counseling individuals and couples, and officiating at weddings and funerals. Anyone who has spent a considerable amount of time in the culture of the church will have been exposed to the functions of the pastor and likely have an opinion as to what his job involves.

Since it is a Scriptural activity, there is much information in the Bible that outlines what God's shepherds are expected to do in service to the body of Christ. In addition, numerous books, articles and papers have been written that elaborate upon the duties and expectations of the pastor. And finally, the well trained minister is one who has Bible school, college or seminary training aimed at thoroughly preparing him for the pastoral role.

If one were to determine the duties of a local church member, however, he would probably be at a loss as to specific and definite information regarding that role and function within the church. The Bible provides much information about who the Christian is and what the Christian should do, but there is nothing that addresses the idea of local church membership.

The view of the New Testament writers was that there was one growing church with believers in the various cities where the Gospel message was accepted. As such, the instructions given to one geographical group were often directed toward Christians in other areas as well. In the history of church development it was only with the rise of different denominations that local church membership took on any meaning at all. As people identified themselves with a specific church, then membership brought distinction. It gave individuals a sense of community and provided organizations with a base for support.

But even then, there is not much information on actual membership, outside of doctrinal practices and beliefs relative to an independent church, affiliated groups of churches or a denomination. Membership classes in most churches consist of merely familiarizing newcomers with the vision, values and policies of the local church. Specific information that may be considered transferable from one church to another is almost nonexistent with regards to the actual duties of a member. Is it any wonder then that many churchgoers approach attendance with a consumer mentality?

The privileges and benefits of membership are the emphasis when one is examining the various options among local churches. These are the days where many select where they will worship based upon the question, "What does this church offer?" The idea of participation and cooperation with a local assembly is secondary to the issue of getting a return for your time and money.

Among the many benefits of membership in a local assembly of believers is the fact that it provides a community or family in which to share and experience fellowship with other Christians. It provides personal access to godly instruction for one's spiritual growth, stimulates faith to believe for God's best in one's life, and is a resource for strength and support in times of pain and trial. In addition, the local church grants a spiritual covering, especially in the exercising of one's gifts in ministry. The New Testament clearly demonstrates the link between one's spiritual development and involvement in the church. There is no doubt, then, that membership comes with certain built-in benefits and privileges, but alongside of them must be the understanding of responsibilities and duties as well.

The purpose of this book is to provide much needed information relative to the function of a church member. The idea of partnership and cooperation with the local church resonates throughout the seven responsibilities detailed here. With the proper perspective of church membership as an opportunity to covenant with and serve the body of Christ through a local ministry, greater productivity in the Kingdom can be accomplished.

The consumer-minded approach to church attendance can be minimized while a deeper level of commitment and service can be arrived at. Every congregation can benefit from a greater awareness among its membership that discipleship is a call to service. God, His church, and our fellow man are to be the objects of our service, and the local church has been designed by God to accomplish that purpose. *The Church Member's Manual* will enable the individual to know exactly what is expected of him or her and to therefore be equipped for maximum productivity in the local church.

CHAPTER ONE: Members Must Support the Church with Their Time, Talent and Treasure

You know about Stephanas and his family; they are the first Christian converts in Achaia and have *given themselves to the service* of God's people. 1 Corinthians 16:15 TEV

A maturing member of the local church will recognize that he or she is not there just to derive blessings and benefits from the church but to be a blessing and a benefit to the church as well. The New Testament offers some practical advice to the believer that can be appropriately applied to membership in the church with regards to supporting the ministry. For example, Paul urges the Corinthian church to pursue unity (1 Cor. 1:10) at a time when divisions among the brethren were jeopardizing the proclamation of the gospel and the stability of the church. His urgent response to their behavior was intended to correct wrong attitudes and put them back on the path to a Christ-centered perspective.

Every member of the local church is important to the body of Christ in general and the local church in particular. The impact of the Christian worldview upon society is dependent, in part, upon each believer's actions in society. And the effectiveness of any local church will be directly related to the level of support given by its membership. The believer should be faithful to the cause of Christ in the world and, as a church member, should be faithful to the local church in its pursuit of the causes of Christ. There are three main areas of support that all individuals are called upon and expected to provide for the success of the local church.

TIME

Membership in the local church requires an investment of that valuable commodity known as time. Attendance at worship services, Bible studies, small group meetings, choir and praise team rehearsals, ministry training sessions and a host of other activities demand the willingness of the church member to be there to participate. In fact, the very nature of the body of Christ is such that interconnectedness and interaction among the various members for the accomplishment of the directives of the body are a foregone conclusion. The presence and partnership of each member is therefore undeniably necessary. The writer of Hebrews speaks profoundly to the issue of church attendance and participation.

> Let us be concerned for one another, to help one another to show love and to do good. Let us not give up the habit of meeting together, as some are doing. Instead, let us encourage one another all the more... (Hebrews 10:24-25 TEV)

In order to encourage and help each other, believers were expected and urged to attend the various meetings of the church. Apparently this statement was stimulated by noticeable absences in church gatherings. Persecution of Christians during the time was perhaps causing some to stay away in fear. Corporate gatherings were the more necessary for mutual encouragement. The early church believers in Jerusalem demonstrated an understanding of the investment of time for both benefit and blessing. Their actions portray a people who were unselfish in their pursuit of the newfound relationship they had discovered in Jesus Christ. Unity, harmony and agreement characterized their attitude and behavior in the initial stages of the church's development and growth.

> And they continued steadfastly in the apostle's doctrine and fellowship, and in breaking of bread and in prayers… And they, continuing daily with one accord in the temple and breaking bread from house to house, did eat their meat with gladness and singleness of heart. (Acts 2:42, 46 KJV)

Every church should strive to possess those characteristics in its membership and every member should demonstrate that kind of commitment. With all of the demands being made upon our time in an increasingly busy society, we should never forget to give time to the things that are truly important and lasting. One's spiritual life and expression should be given priority in the ordering of our lives. Spiritual growth and discipleship include participation in the local church. The giving of one's time enables mutual interaction and development, and enhances the efforts of the church. But the investment of time is not just to support the church with one's attendance but also with one's influence. Influence should be understood here as the positive impact that one's presence and participation will have upon others. As members interact with each other in the local church context, growth and development are stimulated by the influence of each upon the other. Mutual encouragement through testimony, exhortation, worship and even prayer mark the path to spiritual maturity.

> Let the word of Christ richly dwell within you, with all wisdom teaching and admonishing one another with psalms and hymns and spiritual songs, singing with thankfulness in your hearts to God. (Col. 3:16)

> This is what I mean, my brothers. When you meet for worship, one person has a hymn, another a teaching, another a revelation from God, another a message in strange tongues, and still another the explanation of what is said. Everything must be of help to the church. (1 Cor. 14:26 TEV)

> Finally, all of you be of one mind, having compassion for one another; love as brothers, be tenderhearted, be courteous; not returning evil for evil or reviling for reviling, but on the contrary blessing, knowing that you were called to this, that you may inherit a blessing. (1 Peter 3:8-9)

With these considerations, then, the church member is encouraged to show support for the local church by giving his or her time to the various functions of the ministry. Attendance and visibility at the church and in the various programs are one of the ways one can demonstrate a vibrant relationship with God, as well as reveal an understanding of Christian responsibility. Timely, consistent, and committed participation will be of great benefit to both the individual and to the church.

TALENT

The second area of support that a church member ought to provide for the success of the local church efforts involves the exercising of personal and spiritual gifts, and talents. All of us have been endowed by God with abilities that distinguish us from others because of the ease with which we are able to demonstrate them. Some have the remarkable ability to sing, using their voices as an instrument in itself; others have keen minds for organizing and planning; while still others may be gifted in the use of their hands to create, maintain or repair. Without a doubt, every human being has the potential to be good at something and many possess multiple talents. The discovery and use of these talents and natural abilities tend to give us a sense of purpose and satisfaction, especially when they are performed for the benefit of others.

The local church ministry is the expression of individual talents and abilities collectively engaged for Kingdom purposes, therefore the talents of the church member are necessary for effective ministry. In the Old

Testament, Moses was instructed to build a Tabernacle using the skilled craftsmen in the congregation of Israel. His statements reveal an understanding that these individuals were positioned where they were to be of service to the work of God.

> All who are gifted artisans among you shall come and make all that the Lord has commanded...And Moses said to the children of Israel "See, the Lord has called by name Bezalel the son of Uri, the son of Hur, of the tribe of Judah; and He has filled him with the Spirit of God, in wisdom and understanding, in knowledge and all manner of workmanship, to design artistic works, to work in gold and silver and bronze, in cutting jewels for setting, in carving wood, and to work in all manner of artistic workmanship." (Exodus 35:10, 30-33)

The New Testament Scriptures affirm that one's abilities are given by God for the specific purpose of serving in His church. And the church member is to demonstrate responsible stewardship of his gift by exercising it for God's glory.

> As each one has received a special gift, employ it in serving one another as good stewards of the manifold grace of God. (1 Peter 4:10)

> Even so ye, forasmuch as ye are zealous of spiritual gifts, seek that ye may excel to the edifying of the church. (1 Cor. 14:12)

The parable of the talents in Matthew 25:14-30 teaches that believers are expected to use what they have been given and that they will be rewarded accordingly.

> His Lord said to him, "well done, good and faithful servant; you have been faithful over a few things, I will make you ruler over many things. Enter into the joy of your Lord." (Matt. 25:23)

Several things are to be noted from a reading of this parable. First, each servant was given talents that were the property of the master (Matt. 25:14). Whatever abilities we possess do not originate with us but have been given to us by God. If this were not the case we could simply choose our own gifts at will and exercise them. The reality is that if you were not born with some natural proclivity toward singing, then all of the training in the world would never make you an opera virtuoso. You can only work with what you have, and what you have is what you have been given. Hence, we are merely stewards of the gifts or talents that we possess.

Second, each servant was given talents in accordance with his ability (Matt. 25:15). From this we can determine that our responsibilities are to be connected to our abilities (talents and gifts) to manage them. Hence, a person skilled in the use of his hands would probably not fare as well if he were given a task that required administrative oversight. Give him an assignment suited to his natural ability, however, and he will astound you with his precision and craftsmanship. If he has been blessed to excel in both the work of his hands and his mind, being multi-talented, then his usefulness and productivity increases tremendously.

Third, each servant was expected to use what he had been given in service to the master (Matt. 25:19). Our talents and gifts are ultimately for the purpose of glorifying God by using them as He determines and not for our own desires. It is possible to possess a gift or talent and use it selfishly and incorrectly. The text here is instructive regarding the issue, for the one servant buried his talent (put it away as he saw fit to do) and was rebuked for it. At the issuance of the talent it was understood that he was to make good use of it for the master. Certainly his fellow servants carried out their duty and accomplished what was expected. But this one was accused of being wicked and lazy, ultimately dishonoring his master and losing his talent and reward.

Our churches can provide a stronger witness and accomplish the various tasks of evangelism, discipleship, fellowship, worship and ministry when each individual member uses his or her gifts in service to the Lord. In times past the model of local church ministry used to be that of the minister, secretary and a few deacons doing the work, but new paradigms are emerging that promote the necessity of maximum participation for maximum productivity. The Pareto Principle established that 80% of the people do 20% of the work while 20% of the people do 80% of the work. Those figures can be changed to reflect greater productivity from the greater participation of the membership, if "saved to serve" becomes the rallying cry of our congregations.

TREASURE

The third area of member support for the local church has to do with finances or treasure. This involves the giving of tithes, offerings and special monetary gifts to the local ministry effort. It goes without saying that ministry costs money. Buildings, maintenance, missions, outreach, education, training, fellowship, benevolence etc. cannot take place if there is no financial support derived from the members of the church. Thankfully, Scripture speaks to the issue in clear terms and provides a framework within which members can be encouraged to give of their treasure. Just as with the talents that we possess, biblical stewardship affirms that God owns everything, He graciously gives us what we have, He expects us to give back to Him, and He attaches a promise of further blessing for our obedience in giving in accordance with His will.

That God is the owner of all earth's resources is clearly established in the Old Testament.

> The earth is the Lord's, and the fullness thereof;
> the world, and they that dwell therein. (Psalm 24:1)
> See also Psalm 50:10 and Haggai 2:8.

Since God is the owner of everything He is the source of all that we attain or possess.

> But thou shalt remember the Lord thy God: for it is he that giveth thee power to get wealth. (Deuteronomy 8:18) See also Psalm 145:15-16 and John 3:27.

Although God gives to us He asks that we give back a portion of what we receive.

> Speak to the children of Israel, that they bring me an offering. From everyone who gives it willingly with his heart you shall take my offering. (Exodus 25:2) See also Lev. 27:30 and Deut. 16:17.

Our obedience to give as God directs releases the promise of His provision in our lives.

> Honor the Lord with your possessions, and with the firstfruits of all your increase; so your barns will be filled with plenty, and your vats will overflow with new wine. (Proverbs 3: 9-10) See also Prov. 11:25 and Luke 6:38.

There are various instances in Scripture where the people of God were instructed to give for the support of godly initiatives, the functions of the temple or specific tasks.

For the building of the temple: They gave for the work of the house of God five thousand talents and ten thousand darics of gold, ten thousand talents of silver, eighteen thousand talents of bronze, and one hundred thousand talents of iron. (1 Chronicles 29:7)

For the functions of the temple: Bring all the tithes into the storehouse, that there may be food in My house. (Malachi 3:10)

Benevolence for the poor: On the first day of the week let each one of you lay something aside, storing up as he may prosper, that there be no collections when I come. (1 Cor. 16:2)

Each church will have specific opportunities and mediums for the member to contribute in accordance with the biblical standards. These will include tithing, offerings, pledges and special donations. In addition, fundraising initiatives and activities are to be found in abundance in many churches whether it be car washes, barbeque dinners, musicals, cookbooks, bake sales or shopping excursions.

It must be understood, however, that it is the financial partnership of the individual member with the local church that enables the ministry to survive and function. Regular, faithful giving to the local church will result in fiscal stability for the ministry, the continued provision of God in the life of the member, and resources to pursue the fulfillment of the Great Commission mandate to proclaim the Gospel to the world.

MEMBERSHIP ASSESSMENT

- Are you giving consistent, quality time to the ministries of your local church?
- Are you using your gifts in service to your local church?
- Do you regularly give tithes and offerings in your local church?

CHAPTER TWO: Members Must Promote the Church through a Godly Influence and Lifestyle Evangelism

That you may become blameless and harmless, children of God without fault in the midst of a crooked and perverse generation, *among whom you shine as lights in the world*. Philippians 2:15 NKJV

The promotion and advancement of the church in the world is part of God's redemptive plan. Both testaments of Scripture reveal that God calls out a people unto Himself for relationship and fellowship and to reveal Himself to the wider world through that group of people. The church is comprised of those who have acknowledged, turned to and embraced God and His love. The sharing of God's unconditional love and mercy through His Son Jesus Christ to those who have not heard is what enables the growth and progress of God's Kingdom. Every local expression of the church will inevitably seek to fulfill its role in proclaiming and promoting the gospel, thereby advancing the church and the Kingdom of God.

The active participation of the local church in God's plan of redemption is revealed in the Great Commission mandate of Matthew 28:18-20 and Mark 16:15-18. It is realized in the behavior of the apostles who, after Christ's ascension, *"went out and preached everywhere, the Lord working with them and confirming the word through the accompanying signs"* (Mark 16:20). And it is confirmed in the actions of the early church in Acts after Pentecost and after persecution. In each instance they took the gospel message to the various communities and cities that they found themselves in. And in each instance their influence was seen in the many conversions to Christ and the establishment of local churches.

This partnership of the local assembly with God in the promotion of His church is greatly facilitated through the involvement of an informed and willing membership. Alongside ministries that cater to the development of the believer's faith there must be initiatives that encourage members to share their faith, represent God in society, and proclaim the gospel to an unbelieving world. It must be understood by the local membership that it is their duty to engage in activities that communicate God's love to the surrounding community and world.

As the early church believers lived out their faith by honoring Christ and testifying to His Lordship, they were, in effect, promoting the church. As His representatives, believers today are engaged in the same activity. One need not hold a title, position, or ministerial credential to participate in promoting the church. A simple cognizance of your potential to affect a person's eternal destiny, along with a willingness to be used by the Holy Spirit is sufficient to carry out the duty. And though promotion of the church can take many forms, they can generally be grouped into two categories: godly influence and lifestyle evangelism.

Promoting the Church through Godly Influence (in the World)

There can be no doubt that the influence of godly people has had a dramatic effect on nations and people of the world throughout history. Scripture records that whole cities turned to the Lord at the preaching of the apostles in the book of Acts. The same acceptance of the gospel message brought peace and prosperity to those nations that had respect for the church in the early centuries. It can be argued that Spain, Britain and America attained the heights of world dominance only after they submitted to God. And the establishment of numerous social welfare institutions came about through those who sought to express God's love to a hurting humanity. All of this can be attributed to the influential attitudes, perspectives and behavior of men and women who revered God in both private and public spheres.

In His sermon on the mount, Jesus teaches many things concerning the Kingdom of God and its citizens. He gives specific information regarding the behavior that is expected of those who serve God. In many instances that godly behavior goes against popular trend and even personal preference. Rather it pushes one to a level of selflessness and altruism rarely displayed in normal societal interaction. Jesus' statements in Matthew 5 reveal just how valuable and significant His followers are in the world.

You are the salt of the earth; but if the salt loses its flavor, how shall it be seasoned? It is then good for nothing but to be thrown out and trampled underfoot by men. (Matthew 5:13)

If salt is an important condiment and ingredient to us today, it was even more important to ancient society. In biblical times salt was derived from the earth and was intermingled with minerals and vegetable matter. In the absence of refrigeration and modern methods of food preservation it was invaluable in preventing meat from spoiling. In a similar manner the church exists in the world as a preserving influence against the ravages of sin and godlessness. The message and practice of the church always point man to high ethical standards, morality, brotherhood and compassion. Without this message and action countering selfishness, immorality and unrighteousness, the world would be utterly given over to evil.

The church member acts as salt in the world by living a disciplined and godly life among unbelievers. By wholly following God in submission and obedience, he points the unbeliever to a higher level of living. By practicing the principles of his Christian faith he offers an attractive and effective counter to the manifestations of sin and unrighteousness in the world. Paul's encouragement to the believers at Thessalonica, who were being led to believe that the Day of the Lord had already come, points to the preserving nature of the Holy Spirit's work in the world through the church.

> For the mystery of lawlessness is already at work; only He who now restrains will do so until he is taken out of the way. And then the lawless one will be revealed, whom the Lord will consume with the breath of His mouth and destroy with the brightness of His coming. (2 Thessalonians 2:7-8).

Salt was also used as a purifier in ancient times and maintains that quality today. Wounds could be kept from infection by the application of salt. Skin could be exfoliated and cleansed by rubbing with salt. And a mouthwash of salt water could help sores to heal quickly. The church member demonstrates a purifying influence in the world by proclaiming the gospel and leading men to the cleansing power of Christ's blood. The stain of sin is revealed in man's continued rebellion against God and the pursuit of unrighteousness. The only remedy is the applied blood of Jesus Christ as seen in the transformed life of the Christian (i.e. church member).

> Therefore, if anyone is in Christ, he is a new creation; old things have passed away; behold, all things have become new. (2 Cor. 5:17)

Another noteworthy fact about salt is that it penetrates and makes its presence known. The addition of salt to a meal, for example, is generally unmistakable. It has an overwhelming influence on what it comes into contact with. In the same manner, the church penetrates society as each believer/member brings his transformed lifestyle into the workplace, school, business and community of which he is a part. Though he may appear to blend in with his surroundings, the power of God at work within him will inevitably draw attention and provoke a reaction. Believers have been found in every facet and at every level of society, be it education, politics, business, industry, military, music or entertainment. As a result the influence of the church can be felt almost everywhere. Jesus' follow-up to the salt of the earth comparison speaks even more profoundly to the church's influence.

> You are the light of the world. A city that is set on a hill cannot be hidden. Nor do they light a lamp and put it under a basket, but on a lampstand, and it gives light to all who are in the house. Let your light so shine before men, that they may see your good works and glorify your Father in heaven. (Matthew 5:14-16)

This revelation confirms the necessity of the church in the world as the agency of God's redemptive work. The believers who comprise the church are the light of the world. They are the possessors of that light source that dispels the darkness and reveals the truth. As a light bulb turned on in a dark room illuminates and enables one to navigate, so too does the church have the task of showing the way to those who are in darkness. In essence, these verses speak to the prominence, the power and the purpose of the church.

As the light of the world and a city set on a hill, the church is visible and unavoidably prominent. It cannot be ignored or dismissed because it has been positioned where it is in the world by God Himself. Its influence will be inevitable because of its placement. It makes no sense for the local church to confine itself to the four walls of its sanctuary when God has positioned the body of Christ in a place of prominence. Its influence must be felt and seen in the local community by the active participation of its membership in society.

Second, the power of the church is revealed in the function of light. When the light is turned on, those who are in the house can see and benefit from its illumination. As small and insignificant as a candle may seem during daylight, its value and power are greatly appreciated in the midst of darkness. As the light of the world, it is the church that has the power to illuminate and reveal truth. The importance of education, science and philosophy cannot be denied, but it is the church that has been endowed with the influence of absolute truth. That same truth has, throughout history, informed educational, scientific and philosophical pursuits. That's the awesome and undeniable power of the church.

Third, the purpose of the church, as the light of the world, is to illuminate in such a way that men glorify God. Through good works and righteous living among men, the believer points the unbeliever toward God. As representatives of the Kingdom, we are to testify of and give witness to Jesus Christ. We are to honor and exalt Him in all of our ways. In so doing, we are placed on display for the world to see with the intent that the unbeliever becomes influenced to come and join us in the Kingdom and thus give glory to God. A beacon on the ocean's shore points the way to port for the uncertain sailor and results in thanksgiving when the ship arrives safely. The end result of illumination by the church is that men would know and celebrate God.

When the believer (church member) yields to God's design, he can then assume the responsibility of being a proper influence in the local community. His attitude and actions will promote the body of Christ at large and the local church in particular. He will be like salt permeating, preserving and purifying the community and world in which he lives. He will be like that illuminated city on a hill. Men will be drawn to the unavoidable light that he possesses and glorify God.

Promoting the Church through Lifestyle Evangelism

If the end result of the church member's godly influence in the community is that unbelievers come to know God, then it is even more so the direct objective of lifestyle evangelism. This is where believers intentionally develop relationships with unbelievers in order to introduce them to Christ. The relationship provides the context of friendship, confidence, and trust that make the presentation and acceptance of the gospel less intimidating. In fact, the believer lives out the gospel so that his actions, more than his words, communicate the message of God's redemptive love. By providing an up close and personal interaction with the Christian experience, the potential barriers and objections of the unbeliever are rendered ineffective. Out of all the evangelistic methods used in Christian ministry, lifestyle evangelism has proven most effective at promoting Christ, as well as His church, both universal and local. It can even be argued that the growth and proliferation of the church throughout history was facilitated through transformed individuals interacting with those closest to them and leading them to faith in Christ.

One of the obvious and most convenient relationships wherein the believer can engage lifestyle evangelism is in his or her family. Unsaved relatives come with an established familiarity and trust that usually make sharing the gospel easy. The changes in the believer's life that have occurred because of the power of Christ are more readily seen and appreciated by the family member who knows them intimately. The church member should purposefully live out his faith in front of his family and seize the opportunity to demonstrate the Christian life. He should regularly pray for and encourage his unsaved family members to surrender their lives to Jesus Christ. He should invite and bring them to his local church for worship, fellowship and instruction in the things of God.

The Scriptures indicate that many individuals effectively introduced their family members to the gospel by way of their relationship. In the gospel of John, Jesus is identified by John the Baptist as the Lamb of God. Two of John's followers then begin to follow Jesus, intrigued by the possibility that He is Israel's long awaited Messiah. One of them is convinced enough to seek out his brother and introduce him to the Christ.

> One of the two who heard John speak, and followed Him, was Andrew, Simon Peter's brother. He first found his own brother Simon, and said to him, "We have found the Messiah" (which is translated, the Christ). And he brought him to Jesus. (John 1:40-42)

In the early days of the New Testament church, the message of the gospel resulted in the conversion of numerous individuals. Many of them were obviously influential enough to win their families as well. In many instances a family hosted a segment of the larger church in their home for worship, fellowship and instruction.

> Now a certain woman named Lydia heard us. She was a seller of purple from the city of Thyatira, who worshiped God. The Lord opened her heart to heed the things spoken by Paul. And when she and her household were baptized, she begged us, saying, "If you have judged me to be faithful to the Lord, come to my house and stay." So she persuaded us. (Acts 16:14-15)

Greet Priscilla and Aquila, my fellow workers in Christ Jesus, who risked their own necks for my life, to whom not only I give thanks, but also all the churches of the Gentiles. Likewise greet the church that is in their house. (Romans 16:3-5)

Another area for potential lifestyle evangelism to be administered is to be found among the friends and acquaintances that we have. Work, organizational, athletic, entertainment and other pursuits inevitably cause us to develop relationships with people we regularly interact with. Some of them even become close friends with strong ties and lasting bonds. The believer's Christian experience should be shared and freely communicated at some point in the relationship. The church member who is unashamed of his salvation and un-offensive in the expression of his Christian worldview promotes the gospel and the Kingdom of God.

Both the Old and New Testaments command believers to love their neighbors. A practical expression of that love would be to share a great discovery or a unique find with them. The experience of God's redemptive love is the greatest thing one could introduce his neighbor to. The woman at the well of Samaria was so enthused by her encounter with Jesus that she went into her town and told her neighbors about Him.

The woman then left her waterpot, went her way into the city, and said to the men, "come, see a

> Man who told me all things I ever did. Could this be the Christ?" And many of the Samaritans of that city believed in Him because of the word of the woman who testified, "He told me all that I ever did." (John 4:28, 29, 39)

In the days and weeks following the experience of Pentecost the church grew in number as the gospel message was proclaimed both publicly and privately. Luke's account in Acts reveals that in the openness of the Temple as well as in the privacy of local homes, believers shared their faith in Jesus with others. It would not be a stretch to assume that the newly converted freely talked about their decision to follow Jesus with their closest friends and acquaintances.

> So continuing daily with one accord in the temple, and breaking bread from house to house, they ate their food with gladness and simplicity of heart, praising God and having favor with all the people. And the Lord added to the church daily those who were being saved. (Acts 2: 46-47)

The church member can be an effective witness for Christ and His church by becoming an active participant in the salvation of his unsaved friends and neighbors. He should regularly pray for their redemption and look for opportunities to witness to them. He should perform acts of kindness and generosity in demonstration of brotherly love. He should invite them to events at his church that are intended to introduce unbelievers to the gospel. And he should be prepared to personally lead them to Christ.

A third area where the church member can be involved in lifestyle evangelism is in his local community. The local church will have a visible presence in the community and its members should be visible as well. The local school, grocery store, shopping mall, post office, library and a host of other places employ and serve believers who attend local churches. While they may not have full freedom to openly evangelize, they can nonetheless carry the Spirit of Christ with them into those environments. Their actions of integrity, compassion, virtue, and honesty along with an attitude of faith, encouragement and hope will speak volumes. We've all heard stories of people who were turned off from the church because of the un-Christian behavior of members, but what about the attractiveness of those who are truly Christ-like?

> Beloved, I beg you as sojourners and pilgrims, abstain from fleshly lusts which war against the soul, having your conduct honorable among the Gentiles, that when they speak against you as evildoers, they may, by your good works which they observe, glorify God in the day of visitation. (1 Peter 2: 11-12)

> Now when they saw the boldness of Peter and John, and perceived that they were uneducated

> and untrained men, they marveled. And they realized that they had been with Jesus. (Acts 4:13)

In addition to carrying the Spirit of Christ with him to his place of employment or into a place of business, the church member can do ministry in other practical ways. He can volunteer at the local hospital, nursing home or shelter. He can represent his church by participating in family oriented community events. He can lead a clothing or food drive for the needy in his community. He can sign up to coach or referee games with one of the local youth sports leagues. There are numerous other opportunities for church members to get out into the community and advance the Kingdom of God beyond the four walls of the local church.

All that is needed is the knowledge that believers are to intentionally engage their local communities. God's plan of redemption is a work of the Spirit and is made possible through Christ, but its message is given to the believer. In that sense we are true co-laborers with God in His work of reconciling men to Himself. It is a high and holy honor for the redeemed to partner with God in the salvation of their fellowman. Through godly influence and lifestyle evangelism the church member fulfills his role in advancing the Kingdom of God and promoting the church.

> But you are a chosen generation, a royal priesthood, a holy nation, His own special people, that you may proclaim the praises of Him who

called you out of darkness into His marvelous light. (1 Peter 2:9)

MEMBERSHIP ASSESSMENT

- Are you excited about your local church?
- Do you regularly invite people to visit your church?
- How often do you share your testimony with unbelievers?
- Are you involved in community activities where your light can shine?

CHAPTER THREE: Members Must Defend the Church from External Attack, Internal Disruption, and Spiritual Disease

> And they overcame him by the blood of the Lamb, and by the word of their testimony; and they did not love their lives to the death. Rev. 12:11

In a bygone era men full of zeal but lacking discernment took it upon themselves to engage in armed conflict against the perceived enemies of Christianity. It was their intention to regain biblically historical territories lost to foreign invaders who heralded a different religion, and to reestablish Christianity as the beacon of truth and righteousness. Fighting for the cause of God and in the name of God their ventures failed because it was not approved of God. Nothing in the actions of the early church can be seen to affirm a physical and military defense of the church. A holy war cannot be won with sword and shield but must employ other means to secure God's assistance and success.

From its inception the church of Jesus Christ has been engaged in warfare against the enemy of God and the redeemed. Through persecution, intimidation, harassment, criticism and other means, Satan and his forces are determined to frustrate and impede the progress of Christianity. Even though his defeat and our ultimate victory are assured, we are nonetheless encouraged to become familiar with the tactics of the enemy and actively engage in the defense of the church. Our resistance, however, will not be after the manner of men but by the power of the Holy Spirit. The language of the New Testament reveals that we are in a fight against spiritual forces but our weapons are equal to the task.

> Fight the good fight of faith, lay hold on eternal life, to which you were also called. (1 Timothy 6:12)

> For we do not wrestle against flesh and blood, but against principalities, against powers, against the rulers of the darkness of this age, against spiritual hosts of wickedness in the heavenly places. (Ephesians 6:12)

> For the weapons of our warfare are not carnal but mighty in God for pulling down strongholds, casting down arguments and every high thing that exalts itself against the knowledge of God, bringing every thought into captivity to the obedience of Christ. (2 Cor. 10:4-5)

DEFEND AGAINST OUTSIDE ATTACK

The first area of defense for the church is the most obvious, for the threat comes primarily from without. In the early church it was seen in the disapproval of the apostles' preaching by the religious leaders. They faced imprisonment and beatings, Stephen and James were killed for the faith, and Saul of Tarsus spearheaded persecution of the Jerusalem church. But yet the church grew in number and increased in influence. Why? Because the believers did not cower in fear but faced the threat with prayer and a continued witness to the power of Christ.

In the modern era the church is still being assaulted by forces opposed to the truth of the Gospel. Believers in parts of Africa and Asia face overt persecution and worship under constant threat of violence, imprisonment and death. Christianity is outlawed in Communist China but a thriving church exists underground. In the west the assault is against the historical values and practices of Christianity as an increasingly pluralistic society embraces a secular mindset. Even the American church is losing apparent ground to the onslaught of liberal philosophies and political pressure from those who do not fear God. Many in the church have sought to resist these attacks by engaging protest marches, rallies, political maneuvers and public debate. While these efforts may have their merit, there seems to be a more biblical approach to contending against the negative forces that oppose the church.

The incident of the lame man's healing in Acts 3 ended with Peter and John being imprisoned and then threatened not to continue preaching about Jesus. What happened on their release speaks to how we should respond to the external assault on the church.

> And being let go, they went to their own companions and reported all that the chief priests and elders had said to them. So when they heard that, they raised

their voice to God with one accord and said…Now, Lord, look on their threats, and grant to Your servants that with all boldness they may speak Your word, by stretching out Your hand to heal, and that signs and wonders may be done through the name of Your holy Servant Jesus. And when they had prayed, the place where they were assembled together was shaken; and they were all filled with the Holy Spirit, and they spoke the word of God with boldness…And with great power the apostles gave witness to the resurrection of the Lord Jesus. And great grace was upon them all. (Acts 4:23-24, 29-31, 33)

Three things are to be noted here: They prayed for boldness, they experienced the divine presence, and they became a powerful witness. These believers showed remarkable resolve in refusing to be intimidated by the authorities. Their actions reveal that they were more concerned about accomplishing God's will than acquiescing to men's threats. In fact, they went to God about the matter but did not question whether they should continue or alter their efforts.

1. They prayed for boldness: Note that the specific request made by this company of believers was for courage to continue the work of ministry despite the threat of men. They did not ask for God's judgment to be meted out against the opposition; they simply asked Him to see their threats (and deal with it His way). The defensive response of

the church (and the church member) to external assault is to pray that God give the believer(s) courage and fearlessness to live and serve in obedience to His will. Let God answer the attackers in the time and manner of His own choosing. Our focus must not waver from fulfilling the biblical mandate to be salt and light to the world (see Matthew 5:13-16) and carrying out the Great Commission (Matthew 28:19-20).
2. They experienced the divine presence: In response to their request the Holy Spirit visited the place where they were, in a manner similar to Pentecost. The building was shaken and they were given fresh empowerment to preach with boldness. When under assault from the forces of a godless society, we need to find strength in the presence of God. Through prayer and worship and with a determination to do His will, we can experience the Holy Spirit's anointing to face the challenges and overcome. Our own plans, schemes and strength will fail us in this fight. We need the power and presence of God energizing, mobilizing and motivating us.
3. They became a powerful witness: The believers left that prayer session full of purpose and power and it showed in their witness. They continued to preach and proclaim the risen Christ, God confirmed their words with signs and wonders, and the church grew stronger and larger. It was

obvious to all who observed them that this was more than a work of men; indeed the grace of God was upon them. When we boldly live out our faith and allow the Holy Spirit to lead us, we can be a powerful testimony to the truth of the Gospel. Hurting and bound people can experience deliverance and freedom through our actions. Fear and intimidation will cripple our witness, whereas courage and resolve will unleash the power of God in our communities.

This must be our defense against the external forces that are opposing the church today. The church member must not cower at the efforts of the enemy in his own local assembly but respond in the New Testament fashion. Partner with like-minded believers and pray for boldness, be determined to please God by obeying His word, embrace the presence of the Holy Spirit when He answers, and go forth with power and purpose. The church did not survive and thrive through the centuries because believers yielded to the onslaught of the enemy. It grew and progressed because they defended against the assault with more testimony, increased witness and greater power.

DEFEND AGAINST INTERNAL DISRUPTION

The next area of defense for the church comes not from outside its walls but from within its ranks. Differing perspectives, varied opinions and even disagreement will inevitably arise among those who comprise the body of Christ and the local church membership. After all, the church is a gathering of people from various cultures, experiences and ethnicities bound together by the experience of salvation. It is when those differences become divisive and lead to strife and squabble that the witness of the church becomes jeopardized.

    The Bible does not hide instances of disunity and discord among the followers of God. Moses' leadership was challenged on several occasions by both jealous opportunists and the impatience of the Israelites. The nation was denied entry into the land of promise because fear and doubt were allowed to fester against the intentions of God. In the New Testament the disciples of Jesus argued among themselves regarding positions in His kingdom. And the early church had to react to growing disputes between the Greek and Hebrew widows over partiality in the daily apportionment of provisions. Later a council was convened in Jerusalem to answer demands that Gentile converts practice Jewish customs as part of their faith in Christ.

    In His prayer recorded in John 17, Jesus prayed for the unity of His followers and indicated that their oneness would be a sign to the world. The enemy of righteousness has discovered that a multifaceted attack engages the opponent from the outside and from the inside. Internal confusion, frustration and division are very effective at retarding progress or setting the stage for self-destruction. A church that is not aware of these dangers or prepared to combat them will be mired in stagnation and lose effectiveness. Thankfully the Scriptures also speak to the need for vigilance and action against the threat that arises from within.

As mentioned in the first chapter, the Corinthian church was plagued with numerous problems that were dividing the church and marring its witness to the wider community. The apostle Paul gave instructions to correct the attitudes and behaviors that were disrupting the life of the congregation. Among his many directives was the appeal to resist contention and maintain unity.

> Now I plead with you, brethren, by the name of our Lord Jesus Christ, that you all speak the same thing, and that there be no divisions among you, but that you be perfectly joined together in the same mind and in the same judgment. For it has been declared to me concerning you, my brethren, by those of Chloe's household, that there are contentions among you. (1 Cor. 1:10-11)

In Ephesians chapter 4, Paul reminds the believers of their common experience of salvation and the consequent expression of harmony that should be evident among them. In a contemporary culture that promotes self-awareness, self-assertion, and independence, we would do well to heed these admonitions as the people of God. After all, we are members of God's family.

> I, therefore, the prisoner of the Lord, beseech you to walk worthy of the calling with which you were called, with all lowliness and gentleness, with longsuffering, bearing with one another in love, endeavoring to keep the unity of the Spirit in the bond of peace. There is one body and one Spirit, just as you were called in one hope of your calling; one Lord, one faith, one baptism; one God and Father of all, who is above all, and through you all, and in you all. (Ephesians 4:1-6)

Love is a fruit of the Spirit, according to Galatians 5:22, and should be consistently displayed and demonstrated in the church through the believer. Where love exists, the issues that divide and disrupt can be managed and overcome. The church member should live and function with an awareness that love is not an option but a requirement for valid Christian testimony.

> This is My commandment, that you love one another as I have loved you. (John 15:12)

> Let brotherly love continue. (Hebrews 13:1)

> We know that we have passed from death to life, because we love the brethren. He who does not love his brother abides in death. (1 John 3:14)

The Epistle of James provides practical advice for the believer who wants to successfully overcome trials and the temptation to sin. It is apparent that interpersonal conflicts fueled by envy, bickering and gossip were also prevalent enough to warrant strong admonition from the apostle. His corrective response to first century issues is still relevant and effective for addressing twenty-first century realities.

> Where do wars and fights come from among you? Do they not come from your desires for pleasure that war in your members? Therefore submit to God. Resist the devil and he will flee from you. Draw near to God and He will draw near to you…Do not speak evil of one another, brethren. He who speaks evil of a brother and judges his brother, speaks evil of the law and judges the law. But if you judge the law, you are not a doer of the law but a judge. There is one Lawgiver, who is able to save and to destroy. Who are you to judge another? (James 4:1, 7, 8 and 11-12)

If the advice of James is to be heeded and we are to minimize internal church conflict, then the church member should begin by ensuring that he/she is fully submitted to God. It must be a daily, continual submission that characterizes our relationship with Him. At the same time, we are commanded to resist the devil. Do not allow his tactics to seduce us into partnership with his evil intent. Deny and push back against his every attempt by refusing to accept anything less than what God requires. When we do that, we will then avoid judging or speaking evil of each other, which violates the command to love our neighbor as much as we love ourselves. The preservation of the unity and harmony of the church must be our objective in this struggle.

DEFEND AGAINST SPIRITUAL DISEASE

The third area of concern has to do with spiritual disease. The presence of disease in the human body is identified by any condition that negatively affects normative functions. According to the English dictionary, disease is *an illness or disorder caused by infection, diet, condition of life or that is inherited, not by an accident*. Some diseases are classified as contagious or infectious because they can be easily passed from one person to another. Diseases are potentially dangerous because of their ability to disrupt, alter, and even bring an end to life. The response of humanity to the discovery of natural disease has been to fight, ward off, and resist it in its numerous forms.

The issue of spiritual disease is not unfamiliar to the biblical revelation. At various times God's full blessing upon His people had been withheld because of the presence of spiritual disease. Through the prophet Isaiah, God's examination of Israel's condition and consequent prognosis revealed that the nation was gravely ill. Despite their feelings to the contrary they were in rebellion against God and were in danger of divine judgment because they were a diseased people.

> Why should you be stricken again? You will revolt more and more. The whole head is sick, and the whole heart faints. From the sole of the foot even to the head, there is no soundness in it, but wounds and bruises and putrefying sores; they have not been closed or bound up, or soothed with ointment. (Isaiah 1: 5-6)

The prophet Jeremiah drew similar conclusions in his godly pronouncements upon Judah.

> Is there no balm in Gilead, is there no physician there? Why then is there no recovery for the health of the daughter of my people? (Jeremiah 8:22)

> For thus says the Lord: Your affliction is incurable, your wound is severe. (Jeremiah 30:12)

In the New Testament record there is a statement about the damaging influence of sin that is allowed to go unchecked in the church. Paul likens it to leaven that permeates the dough, which lends itself to the same idea of an infectious disease that affects the body.

> Your glorying is not good. Do you not know that a little leaven leavens the whole lump? Therefore purge out the old leaven, that you may be a new lump, since you truly are unleavened. For indeed Christ, our Passover, was sacrificed for us (1 Corinthians 5: 6-7).

On the isle of Patmos John received revelations that were recorded for our knowledge and instruction. In particular, Jesus' review of the seven churches of Asia point to the awesome omniscience of the church's condition that He possesses. The church at Laodicea was apparently wealthy and lacking nothing materially. The economy was good, members were prospering, and life was satisfying. The same could not be said, however, about their spirituality. Among their many flaws was the disease of spiritual blindness.

> Because you say, "I am rich, have become wealthy, and have need of nothing" – and do not know that you are wretched, miserable, poor, blind, and naked – I counsel you to buy from me gold refined in the fire, that you may be rich; and white garments, that you may be clothed, that the shame of your nakedness may not be revealed; and anoint your eyes with eye salve, that you may see. (Revelation 3:17-18)

How do the church and the church members defend against spiritual disease in any of the forms that it may appear? Health practitioners routinely advise us that any effort to maintain good physical health must include a proper diet, appropriate rest, and plenty of exercise. After the same manner good spiritual health may be maintained by a disciplined approach that gives attention to our spiritual diet, spiritual rest, and spiritual exercise.

Our spiritual diet must consist primarily of our interaction with the Word of God. All that we know and believe about God is revealed and expressed through the revelation of Himself in the pages of Holy Scripture. His eternal purpose, perspective, plans and His expectations of us are recorded for us to know, submit to and partner with. For the Christian to grow in a healthy relationship with God, there must be a constant diet of the Word of God that involves reading, hearing, meditating upon, and obeying.

> But his delight is in the law of the Lord, and in His law he meditates day and night. He shall be like a tree planted by the rivers of water, that brings forth its fruit in its season, whose leaf also shall not wither; and whatever he does shall prosper. (Psalm 1:2-3)

> But He answered and said, "It is written, Man shall not live by bread alone, but by every word that proceeds from the mouth of God." (Matthew 4:4)

> As newborn babes, desire the pure milk of the word that you may grow thereby. (1 Peter 2:2)

Along with a steady diet of God's Word fueling our spiritual development, we must also take advantage of the spiritual rest that is ours as children of God. The idea of rest runs throughout the Scriptures and invariably points to cessation or settling down, reposing, or being refreshed. As believers we are positioned to be settled down and refreshed spiritually through our relationship with Christ. Where our salvation is concerned, we are released from self-efforts at redemption and the frustration of failing to attain it. We access it by grace through faith in Christ. And where our living is concerned, we can rest from the anxieties and worries of life by resting in God's providential care.

> Come to Me, all you who labor and are heavy laden, and I will give you rest. Take My yoke upon you and learn from Me, for I am gentle and lowly in heart, and you shall find rest for your souls. (Matthew 11:28-29)

In addition to a spiritual diet and spiritual rest, the believer must be engaged in spiritual exercise. Activities that build us up spiritually and keep us focused on accomplishing God's will in the earth will prevent spiritual disease. Prayer, fasting, worship, serving and witnessing are among those disciplines that promote optimum spiritual health. Every church member should be engaged in consistent participation in these types of activities whether independently, through small groups, or as part of a church-wide effort. The best results come when one combines all three. Healthy growing churches are filled with healthy growing members who are actively engaged in spiritual exercise.

> Is this not the fast that I have chosen: to loose the bonds of wickedness, to undo the heavy burdens,

to let the oppressed go free, and that you break every yoke? Is it not to share your bread with the hungry…then your light shall break forth like the morning, your health shall spring forth speedily, and your righteousness shall go before you; the glory of the Lord shall be your rear guard. (Isaiah 58:6-8)

Let the word of Christ dwell in you richly in all wisdom, teaching and admonishing one another in psalms and hymns and spiritual songs, singing with grace in your hearts to the Lord. (Colossians 3:16)

But reject profane and old wives' fables, and exercise yourself toward godliness. For bodily exercise profits a little, but godliness is profitable for all things, having promise of the life that now is and of that which is to come. (1 Timothy 4:7-8)

The defense of the church is a necessary action that every member must be involved in on some level. Acceptance into God's family also involves enlistment in God's army. The various spiritual threats from without, from within and from disease require vigilant action. The local church can only benefit from congregants who are prepared to resist the enemy's attempts to hinder its witness through strategic biblical responses.

MEMBERSHIP ASSESSMENT

- Are you involved in prayer activities in and for your church?
- Are you praying for and walking in harmony with your fellow members?
- Do you regularly feed on God's Word through personal devotions and Bible reading?
- Do you fast often, witness regularly, and serve in your local church?

CHAPTER FOUR: Members Must Maintain the Unity of the Fellowship through Submission to Godly Authority and Love for Each Other

Behold, how good and how pleasant it is for brethren to dwell together in unity! Psalm 133:1

The unity of the church is to be found in our common experience of deliverance from the power of sin by the blood of Jesus Christ, and the consequent indwelling of His Holy Spirit. By its very definition, the church is comprised of those who have been called out from the world to become the family of God. Believers are tied together by their faith, their testimonies, and their practices. Irrespective of our differences in culture, language, or ethnicity, we are nonetheless undeniably linked in a fellowship of oneness.

Our Lord taught the importance of our unity as indicative of our connection with Him and for our testimony to the world. He prayed, in John 17, that our union would be like His own union with the Father: perfect, unbroken and complete. In the previous chapter we noted the need to defend against the danger of internal disruptions that can divide the church and create discord. Here we underscore the importance of maintaining the harmony that is expected of the church, and is the wonderful experience of believers.

One of the metaphors that is used in the New Testament to describe the church is that of a body. In fact, the church is called the body of Christ, the Lord Jesus being the head. The human body is a wonderfully complex organism with differing parts that function together for the good of the whole. The initiatives that form in our brains are communicated via the central nervous system to the feet, arms, eyes, mouth, etc.., and are executed through a harmonious interaction. A healthy body is one whose parts faithfully function according to their design and thus demonstrate a unity of purpose.

In a similar way, a healthy church is one wherein all of its members are functioning faithfully and cooperatively to fulfill the Lord's commands. It is characterized by uniformity of obedience to the Head and unity in the operation of the various parts. Interdependence and interconnectedness demand an understanding of partnership in the fulfillment of the various objectives of the body. Independence and renegade actions will create dysfunction and adversely affect the entire body. This is why unity must be pursued, achieved and maintained.

> For as we have many members in one body, but all the members do not have the same function, so we, being many, are one body in Christ, and individually members of one another. (Romans 12:4-5)

> And if one member suffers, all the members suffer with it; or if one member is honored, all the members rejoice with it. (1 Corinthians 12:26)

In the local church, the issue of unity is extremely important for effective representation of the Kingdom of God. It is also necessary for the fulfillment of the ministries of the church. The church member needs to be taught these truths and encouraged to do his/her part to ensure the unity of the fellowship. Due to the fact that our unity is revealed in our interaction with each other as members of the church, careful attention must be given to two key areas of relationship. One speaks to the issue of spiritual authority in the local church and the other relates to our love for the brethren.

SUBMISSION TO GODLY AUTHORITY

Throughout the Scriptures it can be seen that God has established lines of authority among His people. For the Old Testament saints, He used priests, prophets, judges and kings to give direction and instruction to Israel. In the arrangement of the New Testament church, God has established a system of authority under Christ and through the enablement of the Holy Spirit. Specific offices are identified and prescribed to give leadership to the body.

> And He Himself gave some to be apostles, some prophets, some evangelists, and some pastors and teachers, for the equipping of the saints for the

work of ministry, for the edifying of the body of Christ. (Ephesians 4:11-12)

Various other titles have been used in the New Testament to designate those who function in ministry. Bishop, overseer, and elder are terms used by Paul and Peter in their writings to the churches of the first century. In each case they referred to those who were in positions of pastoral oversight in the church. They served to instruct, guide, watch over and build up the saints. And because of their calling to these functions those under their charge were to submit to them.

> And we urge you, brethren, to recognize those who labor among you, and are over you in the Lord and admonish you, and to esteem them very highly in love for their works sake. Be at peace among yourselves. (1 Thessalonians 5: 12-13)

> Remember those who rule over you, who have spoken the word of God to you, whose faith follow, considering the outcome of their conduct...Obey those who rule over you, and be submissive, for they watch out for your souls, as those who must give account. Let them do so with joy and not with grief, for that would be unprofitable for you. (Hebrews 13:7, 17)

Contemporary expressions of church leadership vary according to denomination or faith tradition. Some churches are led by a group of elders, others utilize a team of pastors led by a senior or lead pastor, while a large number of smaller churches are led by a single pastor. Each model finds justification in the New Testament account of the growth and development of the church as recorded in Acts and the epistles. Whichever model may be practiced in a given church setting, the expectation of the members of the local assembly is to honor their leadership.

All of the ministries and functions of the local church relate to and serve under pastoral authority. The vision, direction, passion, and effectiveness of the local church are inextricably tied to the office and function of pastoral leadership. And usually, depending upon the leadership style of the local church, the highest level of spiritual authority in the local assembly is vested in the pastor or pastoral team.

Numerous incidents of pastoral and clergy abuses in various forms have created suspicion and mistrust of ministers in both society and the church. Every so often, television, print and other media give front page coverage to reports of scandal-plagued ministries, churches and pastors. Although the offenders are few in comparison to the overall number of men and women engaged in pastoral ministry, the given impression is that most are dishonest. This is a grievous lie that the enemy has successfully manipulated to his advantage in an effort to damage the image of the church in society.

It has also had the unfortunate effect of distorting the relationship between the pulpit and the pew. Some reject pastoral authority based upon past negative experiences that lead to mistrust. Others are blatantly rebellious against any pastoral authority, choosing to live, serve, and worship as they please without regard to biblical order. Like Korah, Dathan, and Abiram who challenged Moses' leadership in the wilderness (see Numbers 16), modern day church bosses assume equality with pastoral leadership and hinder the ministry and progress of the local church. Consequently many churches are losing good pastors who leave because they have been frustrated in their attempts to lead. Chaos and confusion are inevitable in any church whose structure is out of order.

The truth is that most of the men and women engaged in pastoral and other church ministry functions are conscious of their holy calling. While cognizant of their imperfections, they are nonetheless committed to faithfully representing their faith and the Kingdom of God in righteousness. They are committed to living the Word that they proclaim to others. They are dependent upon the Holy Spirit to daily walk in a manner worthy of their calling. As such, they are to be respected, esteemed, honored and submitted to in their respective roles of leadership. Advisory boards have their place but the pastoral leadership is ordained by God as the highest authority in the local church.

The expectation of local church members is that they demonstrate submission to the pastor. As the one ordained of God to exercise oversight in the local church, the pastor must have the willing cooperation of the membership. As he faithfully ministers the word of God through teaching and preaching, the members follow godly directives and practice obedience to the Word. As he guides and manages the affairs of the church, the members work with him in an attitude of harmony. And when he challenges behaviors and attitudes that are contrary to the Christian ideal, they accept it as godly correction and adjust themselves accordingly.

Two of Paul's associates were Timothy and Titus. He had been a spiritual father and mentor to both of them. They had traveled with him and discovered their own calling under his tutelage. As they took on their respective pastoral oversight and responsibilities, Paul wrote epistles to each of them to instruct, encourage and affirm them. He underscored the important role that they each played as leaders of God's church and challenged them to be firm, faithful, and fearless.

> You therefore, my son, be strong in the grace that is in Christ Jesus. And the things that you have heard from me among many witnesses, commit these to faithful men who will be able to teach others also. (2 Timothy 2:1-2)

> Preach the word! Be ready in season and out of season. Convince, rebuke, exhort, with all longsuffering and teaching. (2 Timothy 4:2)

> For this reason I left you in Crete, that you should set in order the things that are lacking, and appoint elders in every city as I commanded you. (Titus 1:5)
>
> Speak these things, exhort, and rebuke with all authority. Let no one despise you. (Titus 2:15)

Unity can be maintained in the local church when there is recognition and respect given by the members to the office of the pastor. As the pastor faithfully fulfills his calling as the shepherd of God's flock, the members ought to faithfully follow his leading as the sheep. The harmonious interaction of this relationship answers the prayer and the expectation of Jesus, the Chief Shepherd, concerning His church. And the local church is thereby positioned for the revelation of God's power.

LOVE FOR EACH OTHER

It stands to reason that if we have been the recipients of God's love we should be able to love others in turn, particularly other believers. His love draws us to each other, connects us, fills us, and unites us. Like siblings, we are joined by familial ties that cause us to be committed to each other. Mutual concern, pursuits and fidelity characterize our relationship. Even though we may differ and disagree on occasion, we nonetheless share enough commonality that we are inextricably bound together. All of this is because of God's love for us. Paul speaks to this point in his epistle to the Ephesians.

> But God, who is rich in mercy, because of His great love with which He loved us, even when we were dead in trespasses, made us alive together with Christ (by grace you have been saved), and raised us up together, and made us sit together in the heavenly places in Christ Jesus. (Ephesians 2:4-6)

Notice how the action of God unites us in the statement. He loved us. He made us alive together. He raised us up together. He made us sit together in heavenly places. What God has done for one of us, He has done for all of us. We are redeemed together through God's love and thus united as the body of Christ, the church. What God commands and expects concerning His church is required of all of us to fulfill just as How we all receive His blessings. John records a specific expectation placed upon the church by the Lord Jesus Christ.

> This is My commandment, that you love one another as I have loved you. Greater love has no one than this, than to lay down one's life for his friends. (John 15:12-13)

The love that we demonstrate toward each other as believers is to be patterned after Jesus' own love toward us. In fact, we see in the actions of our Lord what true love really is. It is selfless and sacrificial. It puts others and their needs first. It subdues its own concerns to address those of another. In the church, we are to have and display a love that is sacrificial. Members ought to show genuine concern and brotherhood as Christ's disciples. Against the self-awareness, self-promotion, self-assertion, and self-exaltation that prevail in our world, we must uphold the biblical standard of humility and selflessness.

One of the biblical ways that believers demonstrate sacrificial love is by sharing their resources with each other when necessary. In the weeks following Pentecost there was such a sense of unity and community that the believers made sure there was no lack among them. They willingly surrendered what possessions they could to care for each other. In so doing the power of the Holy Spirit was revealed in both individual salvation and corporate provision.

> Now all who believed were together, and had all things in common, and sold their possessions and goods, and divided them among all, as anyone had need. (Acts 2:44-45)

> Now the multitude of those who believed were of one heart and one soul; neither did anyone say that any of the things he possessed was his own, but they had all things in common…Nor was there anyone among them who lacked; for all who were possessors of lands or houses sold them, and brought the proceeds of the things that were sold, and laid them at the apostle's feet; and they distributed to each as anyone had need. (Acts 4:32, 34-35)

What we can learn from this is not to establish some communal sect, as some have done, but rather to be aware of our brother's needs and willing to help. Charitable giving to those less fortunate is expected of a prosperous society. And while definitions of prosperity may differ from one context to the next, anytime one has something that he can help another with, he should give it. And believers should especially be predisposed towards helping other believers in need, thereby showing sacrificial love.

> By this we know love, because He laid down His life for us. And we also ought to lay down our lives for the brethren. But whoever has this world's goods, and sees his brother in need, and shuts up his heart from him, how does the love of God abide in him? My little children, let us not love in word or in tongue, but in deed and in truth. (1 John 3:16-18)

Another characteristic of Christ's love is that it is unconditional. It is a love that is motivated by the sovereign decision of the giver and not the merit of the recipient. God does not love us because we deserve His love; rather He loves us despite our unworthiness of His love. We can do nothing to earn or to eliminate His love for us. The wonder of His love is that it is freely given to those who ought to receive His wrath and judgment. It is the highest form and expression of love. It is almost incomprehensible but for the fact that we surmise that God loves us not for who we are but for who we can become. The Scriptures intimate this in its description of a God and a Savior who bestow their love on an unworthy humanity.

> The Lord has appeared of old to me saying: "Yes I have loved you with an everlasting love; Therefore with lovingkindness I have drawn you." (Jeremiah 31:3)

> For God so loved the world that He gave His only begotten Son, that whoever believes in Him should not perish but have everlasting life. (John 3:16)

> But God demonstrates His own love toward us, in that while we were still sinners, Christ died for us. (Romans 5:8)

Our love for each other as brethren must be characterized as unconditional if we are to love as Christ commands. We must love each other without reservation, partiality or hypocrisy. To do that, we must unlearn the world's way of loving others based upon their suitability or acceptability. Instead we must look beyond imperfections, because we're all imperfect people anyway, and see each other as God sees us: in need of unconditional love. In the manner that God loves us, we are to love each other. The love of the believer must therefore be in spite of, not because of. The best that we can become must be deemed more valuable than the worst that we are.

In the local church this is demonstrated in patience, genuine concern, and impartiality among brethren. The church member must show unconditional love by being willing to forgive offenses, pursuing reconciliation when wronged, and promoting peace instead of discord. He must be prepared to allow for differences with his brothers while clinging to the common bond that unites God's family. And since this kind of love is a fruit of the Spirit, he must rely upon God's love to radiate through him. In so doing he will display the kind and quality of love that Paul, Peter, and John encouraged believers to possess.

> Love suffers long and is kind; love does not envy; love does not parade itself, is not puffed up; does not behave rudely, does not seek its own, is not provoked, thinks no evil; does not rejoice in iniquity, but rejoices in the truth; bears all things, believes all things, hopes all things, endures all things. (1 Corinthians 13:4-7)
>
> Let love be without hypocrisy. Abhor what is evil. Cling to what is good. Be kindly affectionate to one another with brotherly love, in honor giving preference to one another. (Romans 12:9-10)
>
> Above all things have fervent love for one another, for "love will cover a multitude of sins." (1 Peter 4:8)
>
> Beloved, let us love one another, for love is of God; and everyone who loves is born of God and knows God. He who does not love does not know God, for

> God is love...Beloved, if God so loved us, we also ought to love one another. (1 John 4:7-8, 11)

The unity of the local church will be maintained through the willful participation of the church member. With the understanding that our unity has been prayed for and anticipated by Christ, we should be predisposed to experiencing it in our churches. Our relationships with our leaders and with each other will determine the level of our commitment to it. Let us not allow the tactics of the enemy or our own human frailties to pull us apart from each other. Instead, let us demonstrate that we are truly one: in faith, in hope, and in charity.

MEMBERSHIP ASSESSMENT

- Are you submitted to the God-ordained authority in your church?
- Do you believe that your pastor has been assigned by God to minister to you?
- In what ways do you show concern for your brethren?
- Are you patient and forgiving towards those who wrong you?
- Is your love for your brethren unconditional?

CHAPTER FIVE: Members Must Honor and Support Pastoral Leaders according to the Bible's Instruction

Receive him therefore in the Lord with all gladness, and hold such men in esteem. (Philippians 2:29)

In the previous chapter we established the significance of the pastoral function and office to the Kingdom of God and the local church in particular. It is one of the five ministry gifts that Christ has given to His church (Ephesians 4:11) for the purpose of bringing it to maturity. And because the pastoral function is likened to that of a shepherd, the pastor is in the unique position of being the leader of the local church. It is his responsibility to lead God's flock to the green pastures and cool waters of God's Word and the Christian walk that will enable spiritual growth and development to occur. And because we customarily honor those whose efforts benefit others, we are to honor, respect, and esteem the pastor.

Numerous instances and verses in the Scripture encourage, reflect, or command the honoring of God's chosen ones who serve His people. In the Old Testament, the priests were to be given special distinction because of their unique service as the intermediaries between God and man. The institution of their function (Exodus 29) was prescribed by God and included careful details and much ceremony, all of which set them apart from their brethren. In the time of the judges, Jephthah and Deborah were both esteemed enough to be sought out by their countrymen for leadership and guidance in times of national turmoil. And the prophet Elijah was fed in a time of famine by a widow who honored him as the spokesman of God. In that instance, her meager supplies were miraculously multiplied because she had faith in his word.

In the New Testament, those who served in pastoral capacities and gave leadership to the church were treated with honor. Both the actions of the people and the encouragement of the apostolic writers affirm the need to esteem godly leadership. In Acts 10, Peter is summoned to Caesarea to meet with a group of Gentiles who are worshippers of God. This divine assignment is orchestrated by the Holy Spirit who works to bring both parties together. Upon meeting Peter, Cornelius, a centurian of the Italian Regiment, prostrates himself before the apostle in an act of high regard.

> As Peter was coming in, Cornelius met him and fell down at his feet and worshiped him. But Peter lifted him up, saying, "Stand up; I myself am also a man." (Acts 10:25-26)

In Galatians 4, Paul reminds the brethren of how they had treated him during his time among them. At the time he was plagued by an obvious infirmity that may have been caused by his labor among them. It was such that they could have disregarded his message and refused to hear him. They did no such thing, but rather received him as they would have received Jesus Himself. They were hospitable and respectful toward the apostle.

> You know that because of physical infirmity I preached the gospel to you at the first. And my trial which was in my flesh you did not despise or reject, but you received me as an angel of God, even as Christ Jesus. (Galatians 4:13-14)

In his third epistle, John addressed a situation that was occurring at one of the churches under his apostolic oversight. An overly ambitious and arrogant individual by the name of Diotrephes resisted the apostle's authority, spoke ill of him, and led others to reject any persons sent by the apostle to the church. Whether Diotrephes was himself a leader is not clear from the text, but what is certain is that he acted dishonorably toward one of Jesus' original disciples who had obvious authority over him, and created an unhealthy atmosphere in the church. John's response is a promise to publicly reprimand Diotrephes when he visits the church, and to encourage the believers to follow good examples while rejecting evil ones. His reaction makes it clear that dishonoring God's leaders should not be tolerated in the church.

> I wrote to the church, but Diotrephes, who loves to have the preeminence among them, does not receive us. Therefore, if I come, I will call to mind his deeds which he does, prating against us with malicious words. And not content with that, he

> himself does not receive the brethren, and forbids those who wish to, putting them out of the church. Beloved, do not imitate what is evil, but what is good. He who does good is of God, but he who does evil has not seen God. (3 John 9-11)

In the local church, it is expected that the pastor will be given honor and respect as God's chosen leader. The position that he holds is such that he should be held in high regard. Prime ministers, Presidents, Sovereign leaders and other heads of state are given honor and distinction among men. Their influence and authority, however, is confined to the realm of men. Pastors, on the other hand, wield influence both on earth and in heaven. They are the ones who have the responsibility to communicate the truths of God's Kingdom to believers, who in turn live out those truths in the earth. They, by virtue of their calling and position, regularly navigate between the realities of the natural realm and the revelations of the spiritual realm.

The work of the pastor in the local church is arguably more significant than the work of other earthly leaders. The efforts of the pastoral office hold implications and ramifications that will outlast this life and extend into eternity. Through the ministry of the pastor, the church member and congregant is prepared for his eternal existence. The labor of political, social, or governmental leaders can only affect this life. Their efforts are directed toward and hold benefit for our temporal existence alone.

Hence, the call of God to the pastoral ministry is a high and holy calling that demands humility, diligence, and faithfulness on the part of the called. But it also demands submission, respect, and honor among those the pastor serves.

> Let the elders who rule well be counted worthy of double honor, especially those who labor in the word and doctrine. (1 Timothy 5:17)

In addition to admonitions to honor and respect the pastor, the Scriptures also direct those who are benefitted by his function to support him economically. The work and service of the pastor to the church is to be underwritten by the generosity and faithful giving of the congregation. It is the desire and design of God that those whose primary labor is the ministerial duties of the church and Kingdom derive temporal benefit from the church in return. Again, this was established in the Old Testament priestly system where God instructed that a portion of the offerings and sacrifices were to be given to the priests. Upon their entry to the Promised Land they were denied any share in the tribal allotment of Canaan but instead promised support from the people.

> Then the Lord said to Aaron: "You shall have no inheritance in their land, nor shall you have any portion among them; I am your portion and your inheritance among the children of Israel. Behold, I have given the children of Levi all the tithes in

Israel as an inheritance in return for the work which they perform, the work of the tabernacle of meeting." (Numbers 18:20-21)

And this shall be the priest's due from the people, from those who offer a sacrifice, whether it is bull or sheep: they shall give to the priest the shoulder, the cheeks, and the stomach. The first fruits of your grain and your new wine and your oil, and the first of the fleece of your sheep, you shall give him. For the Lord your God has chosen him out of all your tribes to stand to minister in the name of the Lord, him and his sons forever. (Deuteronomy 18:3-5)

In the New Testament, the Lord Jesus prescribed that His disciples should be supported by those to whom they ministered. Both Matthew and Luke record the sending forth of the disciples (twelve in Matthew and seventy in Luke) with specific instructions to take no provisions for themselves. They were to anticipate and accept the hospitality offered to them by those who were willing to receive their ministry.

> Provide neither gold nor silver nor copper in your money belts, nor bag for your journey, nor two tunics, nor sandals, nor staffs; for a worker is worthy of his food. (Matthew 10:9-10)

And remain in the same house, eating and drinking such things as they give, for the laborer is worthy of his wages. Do not go from house to house. (Luke 10:7)

In his first letter to the Corinthians, Paul argues that it is appropriate for churches to care for their pastors. In the ninth chapter he points out that the soldier, the farmer, and the shepherd are rightfully given some form of payment for their service. He further reasoned that it was normal and customary for laborers who worked hard at planting and cultivating the crop to receive a share in the harvest. And even the ox was not to be denied the opportunity to feed while treading the grain.

> Do you not know that those who minister the holy things eat of the things of the temple, and those who serve at the altar partake of the offerings of the altar? Even so the Lord has commanded that those who preach the gospel should live from the gospel. (1 Corinthians 9:13-14)

Again it is worth noting that clergy abuses in the area of finances and prosperity preaching have served to discredit the notion that the church should support its pastors financially. Some high-profile ministers with megachurches and celebrity status are notorious for demanding exorbitant fees for preaching engagements. Others have manipulated people into giving large sums of money while expecting a financial blessing from the Lord in return. There have even been instances where audiences have been encouraged to give money in return for a personal prophetic word from someone claiming to have the gift of prophecy.

It is regrettable that some have made profit and material gain their motivation and message in the church. God will deal with those who have perverted their call and ministry, and we should exercise good judgment and discernment with regards to questionable teachings and practices. It does not, however, abrogate the fact that the Scriptures direct the church to underwrite the financial support of the minister.

The wayward sons of Eli, Hophni and Phinehas, perverted their priestly functions by taking advantage of the people and satisfying their lusts, but God dealt with them in His time and in His way. The priestly responsibilities and privileges were not altered or revised because of their bad practices, however. The perspective of the Scripture is that these were rogue individuals who suffered the judgment of God for their behavior. In the same way, the actions of some in the ministry should not be allowed to detract from what God has ordained in His Word.

> If we have sown spiritual things for you, is it a great thing if we reap your material things? (1 Corinthians 9:11)

> Let him who is taught the word share in all good things with him who teaches. (Galatians 6:6)

The support of the church for the pastor goes beyond that of taking care of his financial needs. The work of ministry is tedious and exacting. Pastors, though called and anointed to function in their office, are subject to weariness and exhaustion from the intense nature of their duties. Giving leadership, guidance, instruction and service to the church, along with the varying nuances of interacting with the congregants through worship and fellowship, is no walk in the park. Pastors must constantly battle against discouragement and burnout in the course of ministry. And they must have vigilant people around them who are ready to assist them in a time of need.

This is demonstrated by the occasion of Israel's battle with Amalek as recorded in Exodus 17:8-13. While the weary nation camped in the valley of Rephidim, they were accosted by the hostile Amalekites and forced to defend themselves. The strategy of Moses was to send Joshua with men to engage the enemy while he ascended the hill overlooking the valley to intercede during the conflict. Aaron and Hur accompanied Moses, and their actions reveal why every pastor needs people around him that are sensitive to his needs.

> And so it was, when Moses held up his hand, that Israel prevailed; and when he let down his hand, Amalek prevailed. But Moses' hands became heavy; so they took a stone and put it under him, and he sat on it. And Aaron and Hur supported his hands, one on one side, and the other on the other

side; and his hands were steady until the going down of the sun. So Joshua defeated Amalek and his people with the edge of the sword. (Exodus 17:11-13)

Though the battle was raging in the plain below them, Aaron and Hur were observant enough to notice that the outcome of this conflict was directly connected to their leader. Moses was not up there just to watch, but he involved himself with the lifting of his hands. Aaron and Hur took their cue and looked for an opportunity to assist. The fight was no doubt intense and lengthy, and they saw their leader struggling to keep his hands raised. They were concerned enough to help him, and innovative enough to devise the plan of seating him on a rock and then holding up Moses' hands.

Several things can be learned here. First, every pastor needs someone who will stand with him in ministry, and particularly in times of spiritual conflict. The church member should be willing to partner with the pastor by supporting his efforts and giving assistance when necessary. Second, the church member should be conscious of the pastor's need to rest and recuperate in the course of ministry. Members should make sure that their pastor regularly takes a real vacation (away from ministry), as well as regular times of physical and emotional renewal. Third, as Aaron and Hur came alongside Moses to hold up his hands, the church member should be prepared to supply strength to his pastor.

Finding ways to ease the burden of what he does in ministry may call for one to be an armor bearer, water carrier, or chauffeur to his pastor.

The significance of the two men's actions cannot be ignored. What would have happened if Aaron and Hur had not been there with Moses? How different would the outcome of the battle and the recorded incident have been? Moses was grateful for the intervention of these ready and willing men. Indeed, the warriors on the field, as well as the nation at large, owed them a debt of gratitude. But it could be argued that these men were there with Moses not just because he had invited them to come. They were there by God's design to play their necessary role in the assistance of their leader. In the same manner, the church member is not there to just receive ministry and blessing from the service of his pastor. He has been assigned there to partner with and be a blessing to his pastor as well.

Another way that congregations can demonstrate support is by regularly praying for their pastor. The nature of pastoral ministry is such that the individual is a constant target for spiritual assault. If the shepherd is smitten, the sheep may scatter. If the pastor is brought down or falls, it results in confusion and disillusionment in the congregation. Some weak persons may even turn away from the church and God. Unbelievers and those who are opposed to the church use it to justify their positions. Satan delights in wreaking this kind of havoc in the body of Christ.

In Acts chapter 12, King Herod launched an offensive against the church by having James, the brother of John, beheaded. It was a bold strike against the apostles and followers of Jesus that gave pleasure to the Jewish opposition of the church. What religious persecution had failed to accomplish (Acts 6) they now hoped political persecution would make possible. The suppression of Christ's influence through the preaching of His gospel and growth of the church was their desire. Herod's next act was to have Peter arrested and imprisoned with the intent to kill him as well. What he did not anticipate was the resilience of the church that sprang into action by interceding for the beloved apostle.

> Peter was therefore kept in prison, but constant prayer was offered to God for him by the church…Now behold, an angel of the Lord stood by him, and a light shone in the prison; and he struck Peter on the side and raised him up, saying, "Arise quickly!" And his chains fell off his hands. (Acts 12:5, 7)

The prayerful intervention of the believers enabled Peter to escape Herod's evil intentions. What if they had not prayed? Might he not have suffered the same fate as James? In the same way, Satan has devised various schemes to bring down the pastor, and it is incumbent upon the church membership to constantly cover their leader in prayer. Pray that God shield him and his family from satanic onslaught. Pray that he remain committed to being led by the Holy Spirit in his life and ministry. Pray that he never deviate from or compromise the truth of the gospel. His work and mission are too significant to take for granted, and the church must develop the habit of praying for the pastor.

Paul consistently requested the prayers of the congregations he ministered to. He had developed enough of a relationship with the believers in the various regions that he could anticipate their supplications on his behalf. He had worked with them, had helped establish them, and had given them pastoral oversight. The challenges of his ministry were such that he needed a covering of prayer from those who had benefited from his preaching. They could authenticate his calling and verify the anointing of God upon his life. They would be interested in his continued success. They were the right ones to intercede, supplicate, and petition God on his behalf.

> Now I beg you, brethren, through the Lord Jesus Christ, and through the love of the Spirit, that you strive together with me in prayers to God for me, that I may be delivered from those in Judea who do not believe, and that my service for Jerusalem may be acceptable to the saints. (Romans 15:30-31)

> [Pray] for me, that utterance may be given to me, that I may open my mouth boldly to make known the mystery of the gospel. (Ephesians 6:19)

A good church member supports his church and his pastor too. He honors his leader as God's assigned shepherd for his spiritual growth. He esteems and respects him for his holy office and function. He appreciates him for his gift and calling. He finds ways to stand with and refresh his pastor. He realizes that he is there to partner with his leader in ministry. He ensures that his pastor's temporal needs are taken care of by faithfully giving. He initiates and participates in efforts to be a blessing to his pastor financially. He prays regularly for his pastor and family. He intercedes on behalf of his pastor during times of challenge and difficulty in the church. In all of this, the church member honors and supports the pastor in accordance with the instruction and example of the Scriptures.

MEMBERSHIP ASSESSMENT

- In what ways do you honor your pastor?
- Are you familiar with your church's approach to compensating your pastor?
- Do you practice giving or doing something extra for your pastor?
- Do you regularly pray for your pastor and family?
- How can you be an Aaron or a Hur to your pastor?

CHAPTER SIX: Members Must Work in Harmony with the Local Church Vision through Agreement, Alignment, and Assignment

And I told them of the hand of my God which had been good upon me, and also of the king's words that he had spoken to me. So they said, "Let us rise up and build." Then they set their hands to this good work. Nehemiah 2:18

    The mission and work of the church has been established by the Lord Jesus in the instructions that He gave to His disciples. Most notably, the Great Commission outlines the general scope of activity that should be performed by the church at large. The message of the gospel is clear and undeniable, but how each local expression of the church will proclaim the message and fulfill the mandate will vary depending upon the culture, geographical location, or other considerations. The peculiar specifics of each congregation's method of ministry will be based upon the vision of that church. Founded upon the Word of God and intended to fulfill Christ's commands, the local church vision will give direction to all of its ministerial activity.

    The importance of a vision cannot be overstated. It is a necessity for the maximum productivity of the local church. There must be a clear sense of direction for ministry efforts and a discernible path to achieving the objectives. Congregations that exist without a clear sense of purpose and direction will soon find themselves trying to do everything while accomplishing nothing. A definite vision for the local church will clarify misconceptions, focus endeavors, and validate achievements. Members will be able to know where they are going, how to get there, and when they have arrived. All of the various gifts and talents of the congregation will be used towards the realization of the vision.

The Scripture indicates that the absence of vision is counterproductive. Without a guiding sense of purpose, people tend to follow their own minds. In a church setting, this can be disastrous. What programs will be implemented? Where will ministry efforts be focused? How will funds be spent? These and other questions will plague the visionless, purposeless church.

> Where there is no vision, the people are unrestrained, but happy is he who keeps the law. (Proverbs 29:18)

The establishment of the local church vision will usually come through the pastoral leadership of the church. In the Scripture, vision was usually given to one individual who in turn communicated it to others. For example, the vision to build the ark was given to Noah, and his family followed along. Also, the vision to free Israel from Egypt's bondage was given first to Moses, who then informed Israel and Pharoah of God's intentions. And the prophet Habakkuk was given a divine directive that was to be published among the people.

> Then the Lord answered me and said: "Write the vision and make it plain upon tablets, that he may run who reads it." (Habakkuk 2:2)

Even in the New Testament, the pattern can be discerned both in the behavior of the early church and in the writings of the apostles. The argument that converted Gentiles should be circumcised was resisted in testimonies from Peter, Barnabas, and Paul in Acts 15, but it is James who renders the decision that is accepted and publicized throughout the churches. Later in his ministry, Paul was given a vision that pointed those traveling with him to a specific area for ministry. Further, his instructions to Titus and Timothy set the tone for doctrinal beliefs and ministerial practices in the churches under their watch. And the Revelation message of Jesus through John to the churches of Asia is addressed to the pastors of those churches. In today's church it may be necessary for the pastor to be assisted by the ministers or elders who serve along with him, or even the congregation, in determining the vision. He, however, should take the lead in the process.

AGREEMENT WITH THE VISION

Once the vision has been determined and established through the initiative of the local church pastor or pastoral team, the church member is to come into agreement with that vision. He is to demonstrate an acceptance of the focus and direction of the ministry as determined through the vision process. By so doing he acknowledges that the vision represents God's will for that local assembly. He says yes to the divine purpose that drives the local church's efforts in ministering the gospel, representing the Kingdom of God, and edifying the believer. His entire attitude is to be one of compliance and cooperation with the proclaimed vision of the church.

The experience of Nehemiah in his efforts to rebuild Jerusalem's walls with the assistance of the citizens of the city speaks clearly to the issue of agreement with the vision. While this account is not of a pastor and his members, the principles derived from the cooperation of the cupbearer and his fellow countrymen are applicable to the church context. In the first chapter of the book bearing his name, Nehemiah learns of the distressing state of his people.

Though he held a comfortable position in the palace of Persia's ruler, he was burdened by the news of Jerusalem's state and driven to prayer and fasting. It is in this time of prayer and supplication that he develops a vision to see Jerusalem's walls rebuilt and hope restored to his people. In the second chapter, he gains the support and encouragement of the king to make the journey and carry out the plan. Upon arriving, he assesses the situation, and after three days assembles the rulers and elders of the people to share his vision.

> Then I said to them, "You see the distress that we are in, how Jerusalem lies waste, and its gates are burned with fire. Come and let us build the wall of Jerusalem, that we may no longer be a reproach." And I told them of the hand of my God which had been good upon me, and also of the king's words that he had spoken to me. So they said, "Let us rise up and build." Then they set their hands to this good work. (Nehemiah 2:17-18)

The response of the rulers and elders to Nehemiah's vision is one of agreement and acceptance. His words were encouraging and filled with passion. His testimony convinced them. The support of the king lent authenticity to his mission. And the outlining of his vision was inspirational enough for them to get behind it immediately.

Please note several things from this incident. First, the argument could have been made that Nehemiah was an outsider. He served in the court of Persia whereas these people lived in Jerusalem. Why should they be bothered to support his dream? The truth is that though the people lived in the city, none of them had developed the vision to rebuild its walls. Perhaps discouragement and apathy had set in and they were resigned to their conditions. It was Nehemiah alone who possessed the passion and the plan to address the situation. Consequently, no objection was offered from the rulers and elders to Nehemiah's plan.

Second, the vision of Nehemiah moved the king of Persia to action. It secured his interest and investment. There was an undeniable sense of God's providence in the initiative, and Nehemiah masterfully conveyed it to the elders. No doubt they recognized the truth of his words and were seized with hope and expectation. The potential and possibilities of rebuilding were hard to ignore or dismiss. They had caught a glimpse of the future in that moment, and they were filled with a desire for what they had seen.

Third, they gave both verbal and physical assent to the proclaimed vision. The spoken consensus was that they should *"rise up and build."* But more than just talking about it, they *"set their hands"* to the task. They began to make the necessary preparations to fulfill the vision of rebuilding the walls. It is easy to say yes to good ideas and plans, but it is impossible to show commitment to them without taking action. There must be a connection between what you say and what you do. Agreement with the vision will always be seen in the combined movement of the head, the heart, and the hands.

ALIGNMENT WITH THE VISION

Beyond revealing agreement with the vision of the local church, the church member must also be prepared to come into alignment with the stated vision. This refers to demonstrating acceptance of the church's focus by seeking out ways to help. What role can he/she play? Where do members fit within the mission of the church? How can their particular gifts enhance the ministry's efforts? Again we look to the inspiration of Nehemiah's vision upon the people's efforts to rebuild Jerusalem's walls.

The third chapter of Nehemiah lists the names of the men and various groups that participated in the rebuilding effort. Included among the group are Eliashib, the high priest, the individual priests, the Levites, and others. They all took on sections of the project and put their hands to the work that needed to be done. In fact, there was such a sense of personal responsibility for the project that certain groups or individuals focused their efforts specifically on those areas closest to them.

> Beyond the Horse Gate, the priests made repairs, each in front of his own house. After them Zadok the son of Immer made repairs in front of his own house. After him Shemaiah the son of Shechaniah, the keeper of the East Gate, made repairs. (Nehemiah 3:28-29)

The fact that these and others chose to work on those sections immediately in front of their homes demonstrates that they were completely aligned with Nehemiah's vision. They did not sit back and wait for others to do what was clearly within their own power to accomplish. They took ownership of the vision by becoming involved at the point where the vision came closest to them. A broken-down section of the wall right outside their front doors meant that they would be vulnerable to attack. It would be in their best interest to work at securing those sections where they lived.

The record of Nehemiah relates that the entire effort was so well-supported that they soon had the wall rebuilt up to one half its height. The reason given for the enthusiastic support and quick success was that the "people had a mind to work" (4:6). Their hearts were wholly given to the rebuilding effort. They had not only agreed with the vision of Nehemiah, they had also aligned themselves with the vision. Each individual and family had found a place in the project and lent their assistance to its fulfillment. Their actions instruct us as to how effectively a vision can be realized when each person takes ownership of it by coming into alignment with it.

In the local church, the church member must be determined to find out how he can help to accomplish the vision. He must discover ways in which his unique gifts and abilities can be used towards its fulfillment. He must take ownership of the vision by working hard in those areas or aspects of the vision that are closest to his interests. He must put his whole heart and mind into the corporate effort, knowing that his role is vital to the overall success of the church. When everyone finds their place in the vision and develops a mind to work, the local church will make great strides toward successful ministry.

ASSIGNMENT WITH THE VISION

Assignment with the vision involves acknowledging that it is a God-given directive for the local church. It is His divine instruction for that specific group of believers that together form part of the larger body of Christ. It is their assigned duty or set of tasks that connect them to the overall mission of the Christian church. It is recognizing that the vision represents God's call upon that local ministry. Agreement with the vision states, "This is the vision." Alignment with the vision proclaims, "This is where I fit in this vision." And assignment with the vision concludes, "This is God's work."

An account from Paul's second missionary journey in the New Testament will serve to underscore the significance of agreement, alignment and this third aspect of assignment with the vision. In Acts 16:6-8, Paul is traveling with Silas, Timothy, Luke and possibly others as they attempt to take the gospel into parts of Asia. They acknowledge the hand of the Holy Spirit in their efforts by noting that He forbade and would not allow them to go into certain areas. A clear sense of direction came to them, however, through a vision that Paul received in the night.

> And a vision appeared to Paul in the night. A man of Macedonia stood and pleaded with him, saying, "Come over to Macedonia and help us." Now after he had seen the vision, immediately we sought to go to Macedonia, concluding that the Lord had called us to preach the gospel to them. (Acts 16:9-10)

In this instance Paul's vision was a direct revelation from God. It was not the indirect type of vision, sensed and grasped through prayer and faith, which is the subject of this chapter. The incident is nonetheless instructive to the local church context where the will of God, directly or indirectly revealed, is to be pursued by the congregation. First, note that there was no doubting that Paul had received the vision. The group had spent enough time with him to know his passion for ministry and sensitivity to the Holy Spirit. He was the obvious leader of the mission and had earned their trust. That God would select him to be the recipient of the vision would raise no questions among them. And they were convinced of what he told them because they were convinced of who he was. Consequently, there was wholehearted agreement with the vision.

Second, the group came into strict alignment with Paul's vision. Though they may each have had ideas about where they should take the gospel, they forsook them to give priority to what Paul related to them. Without debate or delay the company of missionary evangelists turned their efforts to traveling to Macedonia. A sense of urgency in their actions revealed their eagerness to fulfill the vision. It can be seen that they literally took ownership of the vision by the statement, *"we sought to go into Macedonia."* Paul may have been the recipient of the vision but it was for all of them to pursue.

Third, the missionary group viewed the vision as their assignment from God. As Paul related the details of the vision to them, they became convinced that God was sending them a clear message. They had been prevented by the Holy Spirit from venturing to other areas and were anxious to know where He was leading. The answer was unmistakable in the plea for help coming from the citizen of Macedonia. God had spoken and they were ready to comply. Luke records that they all drew the conclusion *"that the Lord had called us to preach the gospel to them."* Their perspective was that the vision was something more than an objective. It was in fact their mission and their assignment.

The church member must demonstrate an understanding of assignment with regards to the vision of the local church. He must view it as God's directive for the ministry. It therefore becomes more than a suggested route or plan of action. It is a divinely ordained strategy for the fulfillment of God's purposes for that local church. It is a corporate assignment that demands the agreement and alignment of those who comprise that church. Personal preferences, desires and agendas must give way to the priority of the vision. Through harmonious effort, the members of the church must take the responsibility for and strive towards the fulfillment of the vision. By so doing, they answer a resounding yes to the call of God upon that local ministry and help it to accomplish its destiny.

MEMBERSHIP ASSESSMENT

- Are you familiar with the vision of your church?
- Do you see the vision as God's directive for your local church?
- In what ways do you demonstrate agreement and alignment with the vision?
- Are you fully committed to seeing the vision become a reality?

CHAPTER SEVEN: Members Must Serve and Carry out Duties Primarily for the Glory of God

And whatever you do, do it heartily, as to the Lord and not to men. Colossians 3:23

The Scriptures are quite clear in pointing out that God expects men and women to serve Him. He has created us and given us life and He rules over all of His creation. The functions of nature operate according to His dictates and design. With unfailing regularity the sun rises and sets each day, the seasons change in uniform order, and time passes in weeks, months, and years. Scientists are yet discovering how remarkably systematic and structured the various forms of life seem to be on planet Earth. All of this points to God's orderly establishment of nature and the laws that govern its existence.

Mankind has been declared to be God's highest work in creation. Whereas He spoke other creatures into existence, He put His hands and His breath into the origin of man. And while other creatures function on the level of instinct and impulse, man alone was given the attributes of personality, reason, and free will. It is precisely by his ability to freely choose his actions that man caused the world to be infested with sin and stand in need of redemption. Instead of choosing to obey God, Adam fell through disobedience and rebellion against God's instructions. Though Adam's transgression has affected all of humanity and natural existence, it has never abrogated the rule of God over His creation.

As mankind proliferated in the generations following Adam, he continued to drift further away from God and deeper into rebellion. In Noah's day, Noah alone submitted to the rule of God and obeyed His instructions to build an ark while warning others of impending judgment. After the flood, God singled out a people to represent Him in the earth and point others to His rule and sovereignty. Abraham and his descendants were chosen to be that people to whom God would reveal Himself and establish a relationship. From the beginning they were told to obey, honor, and serve the God who had elevated them to a position of favor and blessing above the other nations of the earth.

> And now, Israel, what does the Lord your God require of you, but to fear the Lord your God, to walk in all His ways and to love Him, to serve the Lord your God with all your heart and with all your soul, and to keep the commandments of the Lord and His statutes which I command you today for your good? (Deuteronomy 10:12-13)

As a nation in covenant relationship with God, Israel vacillated between obedience and rejection of God's commandments. Self-rule and self-determination were often embraced in place of submission to God's reign. Many prophets were instructed by God to warn the people to return to Him and follow His ways. Again and again God revealed that He expected Israel, and indeed all of mankind, to pursue His will in their interaction with each other and their service to Him.

> He has shown you, O man, what is good; and what does the Lord require of you but to do justly, to love mercy, and to walk humbly with your God? (Micah 6:8)

The book of Ecclesiastes records Solomon's pursuit of meaning in life though the experience of every desire and pleasure. He carefully observed and noted the various nuances of human existence, often remarking that all was vanity. His concluding statements reveal that mankind's purpose for existence was not to be found in the self-centered experiences that mark many who live only for their own enjoyment and achievement. Rather man's life is to be properly lived with God at the center.

> Let us hear the conclusion of the whole matter: Fear God, and keep his commandments: for this is the whole duty of man. (Ecclesiastes 12:13 KJV)

In the New Testament, Jesus reiterates the idea of man needing to live life in accordance with God's expectation. Matthew 22 records an attempt by the Pharisees to entrap Jesus in His teachings hoping that He would say something politically incriminating against Caesar. When their scheme failed they again questioned him to identify the one great commandment in the Law of Moses.

> Jesus said to him, "You shall love the Lord your God with all your heart, with all your soul, and with all your mind. This is the first and great commandment. And the second is like it: You shall love your neighbor as yourself." (Matthew 22:37-39)

If God expects men in general to serve Him and to carry out His will, then it is even more expected of those who comprise His church. The redeemed are those who have responded to God's offer and provision of salvation from sin. They have acknowledged His sovereignty and surrendered their lives to the Lordship of Christ. They have become participants in the proclamation of the gospel and the advancement of the kingdom of God on the earth. All that is done in ministry, as well as one's personal walk, is to be aimed at honoring and pleasing God. Though He calls, equips, and empowers men in the carrying out of His will, it must be remembered that it is His will and not our own. In the local church we are to serve and function for God's glory.

In Colossians chapter three, the apostle Paul points the believer to the type of character traits and behavior that should be seen in the redeemed. He acknowledges that prior to conversion they had exhibited ungodly behavior, but now they were to actively pursue righteous conduct. He repeatedly points them to God and Christ in the working out of their relationships with each other. They are told to forgive as Christ forgave, to give way to the rule of God's peace in their hearts, to be indwelt with the wisdom of Christ's Word, and to sing from their hearts to the Lord. The statement of verse 17 sums up the idea that all of their efforts are to be undertaken primarily for the glory of God.

> And whatever you do in word or deed, do all in the name of the Lord Jesus, giving thanks to God the Father through Him. (Colossians 3:17)

The physical action and verbal expression of the church member is to be directed towards honoring Christ. As he serves among his brethren in the local church, the member is to ensure that his motives are in line with his Lord's expectations. The name of Jesus must be cast in a good light by the behavior of the members of the church. The worth, dignity, and power of that name must be affirmed in worship, service, fellowship and ministry. In so doing, the member demonstrates appreciation to God for the gift of His Son.

A similar sentiment is expressed in Paul's directive to bondservants who were Christians in the Colossian churches. While not meant to approve of their status as slaves, the advice seeks to encourage them to glorify God even in the position that they held. They were to see their labor as unto the heavenly Master as opposed to earthly men. The instruction is applicable to the believer and church member who labors in the workplace and in the local church. Keeping God in view is a greater motivation to wholehearted service than seeking man's approval.

> And whatever you do, do it heartily, as to the Lord and not to men, knowing that from the Lord you will receive the reward of the inheritance; for you serve the Lord Christ. (Colossians 3:23-24)

Peter's first epistle also directs the believer to the idea of serving for God's glory. He opens the first chapter by recounting the hope that the Christian possesses because of God's mercy revealed through Christ Jesus. The particular believers to whom he writes were facing trials and persecution in the first century, yet they could rejoice in God's providential care and protection. The hope of their salvation was a source of motivation to live obedient and holy lives before God. Submission to governing authorities, to earthly masters, to each other, and even suffering for righteousness could be better managed by the knowledge that Christ also submitted and suffered. In the fourth chapter Peter reminds them that the end of all things is near and that they should demonstrate love and hospitality towards each other. Then he exhorts them regarding their service.

> As each one has received a gift, minister it to one another, as good stewards of the manifold grace of God. If anyone speaks, let him speak as the oracles of God. If anyone ministers, let him do it as with the ability which God supplies, that in all things God may be glorified through Jesus Christ, to whom belong the glory and the dominion forever and ever. Amen. (1 Peter 4:10-11)

Several things of note in Peter's instruction will aid the church member in serving in the proper manner and with the proper motive. First, each one who possesses a gift must recognize that it was given to them by God. It did not originate with them but was placed in them by the grace of God. As such, the individual must responsibly manage or be a good steward of the gift. He must know that he is being held accountable by God for how he uses what he has been given. Stewardship comes with accountability and demands responsibility.

Next, the individual must use his gift in service to his fellow believers. He is to minister to those who will benefit from the exercise of the gift. The gift is not given for personal use, gratification, or exaltation but for the support of others in the church. Teaching, singing, administrating and helping are all intended for the benefit of the recipient. The church is built up, edified, and strengthened when the church member uses his gift to serve the Kingdom of God. There is then a natural interconnectedness that is realized in the presence of gifts in the church. The gifted member needs the church so that he has a place within which to exercise his gift and demonstrate responsibility to his Lord. The church needs the member's gift in order to benefit from the comfort, instruction, and inspiration that it brings.

Then, the exercise of the gift by the church member must be empowered by the Lord. Peter says one must speak as the oracle of God. He must speak as the very utterance of God, which means that he must allow

God to speak through him. The preacher/teacher must be conscious of his status as a vessel that the Holy Spirit desires to use. Submission to and reliance upon the Holy Spirit in the preparation and the presentation will result in the utterance of God. Ministry must be done with a dependence upon divine ability. Human strength and resources are insufficient and vastly inferior to the demand of heavenly work. Though God uses human instruments, they stand in need of His divine empowerment to be effective. The power of the Holy Spirit is available in the exercise of our gifts so that we may accomplish spiritually what cannot be done naturally.

Finally, Peter's exhortation hints that in the successful exercise of our gifts we should take no credit for ourselves but give all the glory to God. It is a powerful temptation for us to bask in the wonder of incredible accomplishment as if we did it entirely on our own. The admiration and adulation that others may heap upon us can be intoxicating. But we must always remember that we can do nothing without Christ's power through the Holy Spirit. He may have worked through us to benefit others, but the praise and honor ultimately belong to Him. The end result of ministry and service in the church by those gifted is that God may be glorified through Christ Jesus.

The church member must demonstrate a keen understanding of his responsibility to serve in the church for the glory of God. The assigned duties and responsibilities may seem small and insignificant compared to others but they are all necessary. God has positioned us where He wants us to be in Christ's body. He has also given us whatever gifts and abilities that we possess to be of service to the Kingdom. The church member will be effective when he serves as unto the Lord and not as unto men. He will demonstrate good stewardship of his gifts by ministering to others with a dependence upon the Holy Spirit. He will take no credit for his successes but will direct and deflect all the glory to God.

MEMBERSHIP ASSESSMENT

- Do you prefer to work in the spotlight or behind the scenes?
- Do you believe that God will judge you for your service as a believer?
- Are you fulfilled in your service to your church?
- Are you using all of your gifts in service to your church?
- How is God being glorified by your service to your local church?

CONCLUSION

The importance of the local church cannot be understated. The Church universal is present and influential throughout the world through the collective efforts of local communities of faith. The members of the local church are the faces, the hands, the feet, and the voices that make up the body of Christ in a given community. Who Jesus is and what He represents will be revealed in the actions and attitudes of the church member.

If the return of Christ is to gather a perfected church, should we not make every effort to do our part in pursuing perfection? God's best and ultimate for us should be our aim. Individually that means becoming and achieving all that God has designed for us. At home, at work, in the community, and in the church we should strive to be and do all that God has instructed in His word. The world needs good people. It needs good husbands and wives, fathers and mothers, sons and daughters. It needs good employees and employers, laborers and managers, businessmen and craftsmen. The world needs good citizens living in and comprising its towns, cities, states and countries. And the world needs good church members submitted to God, reflecting Christ, and empowered by the Holy Spirit.

Good church membership could ideally result when mature believers carry out the mission of the Kingdom through the local church. The reality is, however, that Christian maturity is an ongoing process that requires daily diligence and attention. The believer who walks with His Lord one day at a time and is provided stimulation to grow in the local church will make progress. In the same manner good church membership will be cultivated by intentional teaching and training that points the believer towards godly responsibility.

If the local church and believer are necessary to the overall mission of the Kingdom of God then the church member is vital to the local church's participation. Good local churches are made up of good local church members. Good church members are maturing believers who understand their responsibilities as citizens of God's Kingdom. They are committed to the collective efforts of the local assembly and have been taught how to serve in their local church. May these principles and strategies form an invaluable guide to the productive service of your membership in your local church.